SPELLING

YEAR

PASCAL
PRESS

Reading Eggspress Spelling Workbook – Year 3

Reprinted 2016, 2020, 2021, 2022, 2023, 2024

ISBN: 978-1-74215-308-7

Distrbuted by:
Pascal Press
PO Box 250
Glebe NSW 2037

Ph: (02) 9198 1748

Website: www.pascalpress.com.au

Publisher: Katy Pike
Series editor: Amy Russo
Editors: Laura Anderson, Stacey Belgre
Designed and typeset by The Modern Art Production Group
Printed in China by 1010 Printing International Ltd

CONTENTS

WHAT IS READING EGGSPRESS?

Reading Eggspress is an online program designed to build language and literacy skills for students in Years 1–6. The program has targeted lesson sequences for Comprehension and Spelling that align with national curriculum standards for achievement. With built-in rewards, access to over 4000 e-books and rich assessment data to track progress, the Reading Eggspress program individualises learning to help students achieve their personal best.

How does the Reading Eggspress Spelling Program work?

Research proves that students have more spelling success if they learn to recognise common spelling patterns and generalisations as part of an explicit and systematic teaching program. The *Reading Eggspress Spelling program* focuses on common spelling rules, generalisations and strategies using a combination of teaching videos, engaging online activities, games and tests with fully integrated student books.

The *Reading Eggspress Spelling books* for Years 1–6 extend students as they learn, use and apply their spelling skills across a range of written activities. The student books work alongside the online program to reinforce learning for each lesson.

The *Reading Eggspress Spelling program* is structured to provide instruction on a spelling rule, strategy or generalisation with 36 lessons per year level. Each lesson is centred on a carefully crafted word list, based around the sound, structure or meaning features of words. These word lists have been created by consulting educational research and the Australian Curriculum.

Self-paced systematic program

Easy to understand videos

Assessment and instant feedback

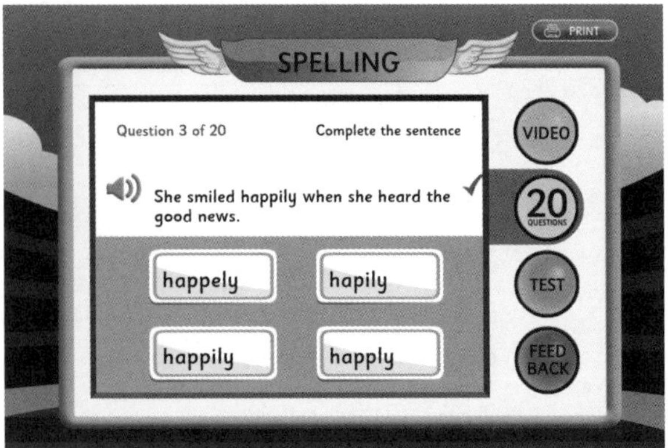

Practice activities

Spelling and the Australian Curriculum

Each lesson focuses on a core set of 20 words and 10 challenge words. These lists align with the Australian Curriculum Content Descriptions.

Literacy

Phonic and word knowledge

- understand how to apply knowledge of phoneme–grapheme (sound–letter) relationships, syllables, and blending and segmenting to fluently read and write multisyllabic words with more complex letter patterns (AC9E3LY09)
- understand how to apply knowledge of common base words, prefixes, suffixes and generalisations for adding a suffix to a base word to read and comprehend new multimorphemic words (AC9E3LY10)
- use phoneme–grapheme (sound–letter) relationships and less common letter patterns to spell words (AC9E3LY11)
- recognise and know how to write most high-frequency words including some homophones (AC9E3LY12)

Language

Language for expressing and developing ideas

- understand that apostrophes signal missing letters in contractions, and apostrophes are used to show singular and plural possession (AC9E3LA11)

Reading Eggspress Spelling

Each lesson uses a combination of activities from the following categories:

Proofreading: self-directed checking of written text. Proofreading assists the development of reading and writing.

Visual memory: the Look-say-cover-write-check creates a visual memory of the word. It is important as a self-correction skill.

Definitions: morphemic understanding of words. This skill is used selectively where an understanding of the etymology and morphological structure benefits orthographic understanding.

Word families: groups of words that share common morphemes. Identifying visual and morphemic commonalities aids accurate spelling and is used throughout the program.

Word sorts: groups of words that share a common theme. Word sorts have been integrated as grouping together like ideas helps learners make sense of the world around them.

Overview of Spelling Aspects Covered in Year 3

Spelling Aspect	Areas Covered	Pages
Digraphs and trigraphs	shr, thr; oy, oi; air, eer; igh; wh, ph, gh; squ, sph; ear	4, 5, 8, 9, 12, 13, 20, 21, 36, 37, 56, 57, 66, 67
Endings	et, it, ot; ch, tch; le, el, al; ery, ary, ory	6, 7, 10, 11, 26, 27, 48, 49
Prefixes	un, dis, mis	68, 69
Suffixes	s, es; ing; ed; er, or; ies, ied; ed; ful, less; y; ly; ness	14, 15, 18, 19, 22, 23, 28, 29, 34, 35, 38, 39, 42, 43, 50, 51, 58, 59, 64, 65, 72, 73
Letter patterns	augh, ough; ei, ey, eigh	24, 25, 40, 41
Other aspects of spelling	vowels; silent letters; homophones; soft c and g; past tense verbs; compound words; contractions; irregular plurals; tricky words	2, 3, 16, 17, 30, 31, 32, 33, 44, 45, 46, 47, 52, 53, 54, 55, 60, 61, 62, 63, 70, 71

MY PROGRESS CHART • LESSONS 3.1 – 3.18

Name ____

Lesson	Level	Online test score	Pages	Self-assessment *With this list I feel ...*
3.1 Short and long vowel sounds		/10	2–3	
3.2 shr and thr words		/10	4–5	
3.3 Word endings – et, it, ot		/10	6–7	
3.4 Vowel sounds – oy and oi		/10	8–9	
3.5 Words with the ch sound		/10	10–11	
3.6 Trigraphs – air and eer		/10	12–13	
3.7 Plurals – s, es		/10	14–15	
3.8 Silent letters – b, l, h		/10	16–17	
3.9 Suffixes – ing		/10	18–19	
3.10 Vowel trigraph – igh		/10	20–21	
3.11 Suffixes – ing with short vowels		/10	22–23	
3.12 Words with the same end sound – ei, ey and eigh		/10	24–25	
3.13 Word endings – le, el, al		/10	26–27	
3.14 Suffixes – ed		/10	28–29	
3.15 Homophones		/10	30–31	
3.16 Silent letters – k, g, w		/10	32–33	
3.17 Suffixes – er, or		/10	34–35	
3.18 Consonant digraphs – wh, ph, gh		/10	36–37	

MY PROGRESS CHART • LESSONS 3.19 - 3.36

Name ______________________________

Lesson	Level	Online test score	Pages	Self-assessment *With this list I feel ...*
3.19 Suffixes – ies, ied		/10	38–39	
3.20 Spelling patterns – augh, ough		/10	40–41	
3.21 Suffixes ed – with short vowels		/10	42–43	
3.22 Soft c and g		/10	44–45	
3.23 Irregular verbs – past tense		/10	46–47	
3.24 Word endings – ary, ery and ory		/10	48–49	
3.25 Suffixes – ful and less		/10	50–51	
3.26 Silent letters – t, n, u		/10	52–53	
3.27 Compound words		/10	54–55	
3.28 squ, sch and sph words		/10	56–57	
3.29 Suffixes – y		/10	58–59	
3.30 Contractions		/10	60–61	
3.31 Irregular Plurals		/10	62–63	
3.32 Suffixes – ly		/10	64–65	
3.33 Trigraph – ear		/10	66–67	
3.34 Prefixes – un, dis, mis		/10	68–69	
3.35 Tricky words		/10	70–71	
3.36 Suffixes – ness		/10	72–73	

Short and long vowel sounds

List

1 Write the word.

map ______
name ______
egg ______
mine ______
lid ______
log ______
cute ______
sum ______
mole ______
mule ______
glad ______
slime ______
frog ______
black ______
lump ______
flame ______
sink ______
apple ______
fled ______
stole ______

2 In a group. Write the list word that belongs in each group.

horse, donkey, ______

atlas, chart, ______

tap, plug, ______

run, escaped, ______

wood, tree, ______

bump, bulge, ______

white, grey, ______

goo, slippery, ______

happy, pleased, ______

pear, orange, ______

3 Fill in the missing vowels.

n ___ m ___

m ___ l ___

l ___ mp

m ___ n ___

st ___ l ___

c ___ t ___

mol ___

s ___ m

4 Name.

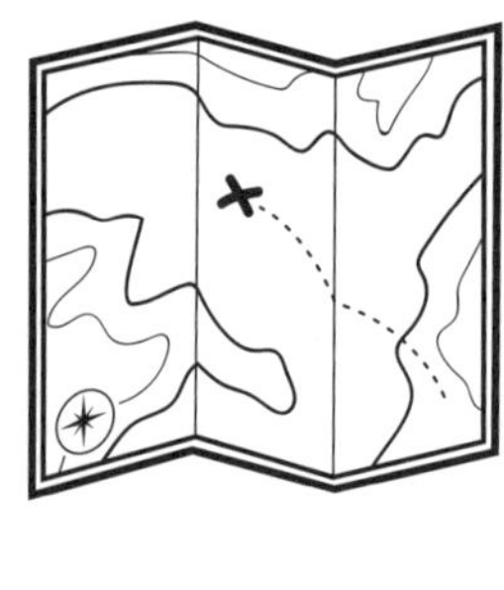

______

______

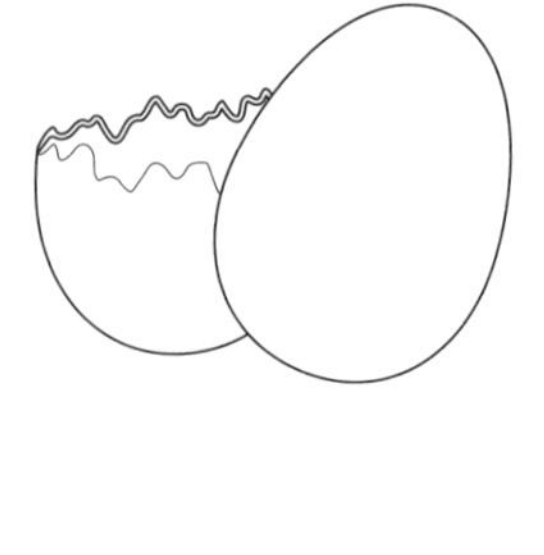

______

______

Short and long vowel sounds

5 Fill in the missing words.

The ____________ of Shelley's friend is Marko.

I cracked the ____________ into the mixing bowl.

That's not your jumper, it's ____________.

You should always put the ____________ back on the jam jar.

Down by the water I could hear a ____________ croak.

The ____________ of the fire was so hot it warmed the whole house.

I was upset when someone ____________ my bike.

The ____________ dug a deep tunnel underground.

That puppy is very ____________.

Challenge words

6 Write the word.

spend ____________
white ____________
crest ____________
tiger ____________
smash ____________
quake ____________
hind ____________
plume ____________
extreme ____________
behave ____________

7 Complete the sentence.

She counted six ____________ fluffy clouds.

The ____________ stalked its prey through the jungle.

Our house suffered damage during the ____________.

The cockatoo has a large yellow ____________.

Mum said if we didn't ____________ there would be trouble.

The bird flew off, but left a white ____________ behind.

I didn't want to ____________ the rest of my pocket money in the same day.

The ____________ from the car accident outside woke me up.

8 Another way to say it. Which challenge word could replace the underlined word?

He has a <u>feather</u> in his hat. ____________

The dog stood on its <u>back</u> legs. ____________

Hang gliding is an <u>intense</u> sport. ____________

She is trying not to <u>use</u> all her money. ____________

I hope the ball doesn't <u>break</u> the window. ____________

shr and thr words

List

1 Write the word.

shred ____________
three ____________
shrub ____________
throw ____________
shrug ____________
threw ____________
shrill ____________
throb ____________
throne ____________
thrill ____________
shrine ____________
thrive ____________
shrink ____________
thrash ____________
throng ____________
shrunk ____________
thrust ____________
shrimp ____________
thrush ____________
thresh ____________

2 Word clues. Which list word matches?

short tree ____________
a place for worship ____________
push with force ____________
a type of bird ____________
beat or pulse strongly ____________
crowd of people ____________
shoulder movement ____________
tear into little pieces ____________

3 *shr* words

____________ ____________
____________ ____________
____________ ____________
____________ ____________

***thr* words**

____________ ____________
____________ ____________
____________ ____________
____________ ____________
____________ ____________
____________ ____________

4 Complete the word with *shr* or *thr*.

___ ___ ___ ow

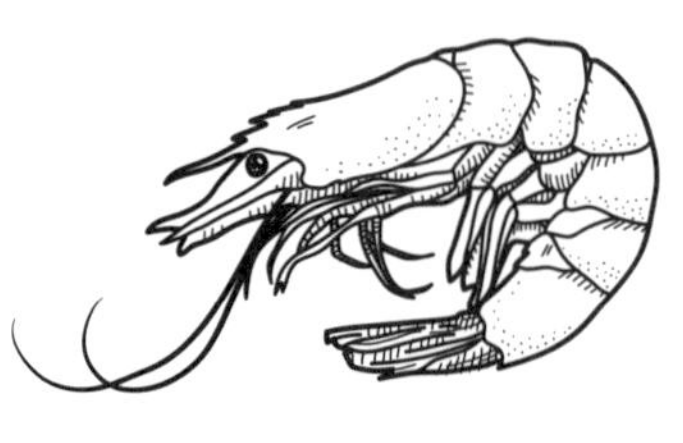

___ ___ ___ imp

___ ___ ___ ush

___ ___ ___ one

5 Underline the spelling mistake. Write the word correctly.

My shirt had shrenk in the wash. ____________

The king sat upon his throwne. ____________

I throo my jumper into my bag. ____________

The sum of one and two is thri. ____________

I chred the paper into tiny pieces. ____________

Riding a roller-coaster is such a threll. ____________

The schrubb Mum planted is growing quickly. ____________

Please thro that brown parcel to me. ____________

The seedlings I planted are beginning to thryve. ____________

Challenge words

6 Write the word.

throat ____________

through ____________

shriek ____________

thread ____________

shrewd ____________

throttle ____________

shroud ____________

shrivel ____________

shrapnel ____________

enthrone ____________

7 Hidden words. Find the challenge word.

thshrthroatthrgh ____________

shrooshrapnelshror ____________

throughshrou ____________

shrapthrottlesh ____________

hruenthrone ____________

rshrouthreadoeiu ____________

heerrshrewdasshs ____________

enthrenthronenneeh ____________

shseeshrieksshrei ____________

8 Another way to say it. Which challenge word could replace the underlined word?

The girl let out a loud <u>yelp</u> of excitement. ____________

The flowers could <u>wilt</u> and die in the hot sun. ____________

My brother made a <u>clever</u> move to get closer to the cake. ____________

Tamara had a loose <u>strand</u> hanging from her jumper. ____________

The bird flew <u>among</u> the trees. ____________

A thick <u>veil</u> of fog rolled down the valley. ____________

Word endings – et, it, ot

List

market
secret
pocket
jacket
basket
planet
blanket
visit
rabbit
carrot
target
cricket
wallet
bullet
trumpet
helmet
submit
bandit
profit

1 Write the word.

2 Chunks. Rearrange the letters to make a list word.

rk ma et ______	an bl ket ______
et ck ja ______	rr ot ca ______
it bb ra ______	sk ba et ______
um tr pet ______	lm et he ______

3 Meaning. Which list word means?

a person who steals from people who are travelling ______

to give in to someone or something ______

when money made is more than money spent ______

an object an arrow is shot at ______

a place where goods are bought and sold ______

something private, not told to others ______

4 Complete the list words.

helm ___ ___
band ___ ___
carr ___ ___
targ ___ ___
rabb ___ ___
trump ___ ___
subm ___ ___
crick ___ ___

5 Name.

______

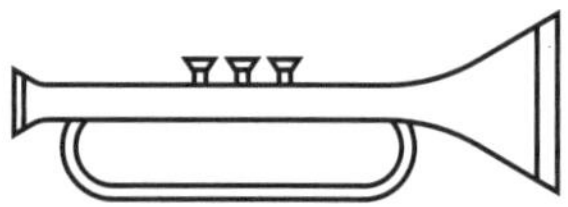
______

______

______

Word endings – et, it, ot

6 Complete each sentence with a list word.

I put my purse in the ______________ of my pants.

Our ______________ revolves around the sun.

I wear a ______________ when the weather is cold.

We put the food in a shopping ______________.

The arrow just missed its ______________.

I went to the ______________ to buy fruit and vegetables.

I fed the horse a ______________.

When it is cold I put an extra ______________ on my bed.

Challenge words

7 Write the word.

poet ______________

quiet ______________

diet ______________

budget ______________

cabinet ______________

permit ______________

deposit ______________

inherit ______________

summit ______________

maggot ______________

8 Word clues. Which challenge word matches?

a person who writes poetry ______________

the food eaten by a person or animal ______________

a grub that turns into a fly ______________

opposite to noisy ______________

the highest part, the peak ______________

to allow ______________

9 Another way to say it. Which challenge word could replace the underlined word?

The climber reached the <u>top</u> of the mountain. ______________

Mum went to the bank to <u>put</u> money into my account. ______________

We keep our cups in the <u>cupboard</u>. ______________

Toby will <u>receive</u> his dad's favourite watch. ______________

Our teacher does not <u>allow</u> talking during class. ______________

Tessa made a <u>plan</u> to help her save money. ______________

Vowel sounds – oy and oi

List **1 Write the word.**

oil __________
boy __________
boil __________
toy __________
coin __________
joy __________
soil __________
toil __________
point __________
joint __________
avoid __________
enjoy __________
noise __________
voice __________
annoy __________
royal __________
foyer __________
loyal __________
spoil __________
convoy __________

2 Fill in the missing list word.

We have to __________ the water to cook spaghetti.

The baby was excited to play with his new __________.

We really __________ going to the beach.

Fruit left too long on the tree will __________.

We planted seeds in the __________.

I put a __________ in the vending machine.

I tried to __________ getting sunburnt by putting on sunscreen.

I like to sing in a really loud __________.

There was a strange __________ coming from outside.

The Queen is part of the __________ family.

We waited in the __________ of the hotel.

3 Fill in the missing letters.

___ oye ___

p ___ ___ nt

a ___ o ___ d

an ___ ___ y

lo ___ ___ ___

joi ___ ___

t ___ ___ l

o ___ l

4 Name.

____

____

____

____

Vowel sounds – oy and oi

4 Underline the spelling mistake. Write the word correctly.

He tossed his last coyn into the wishing well. ______

Getting full marks on her assignment gave her much joi. ______

The workers had to toyle all day under the hot sun. ______

I tried to poynt the traveller in the right direction. ______

The tennis player hurt her elbow joynt. ______

I tried to avoyd Monday by staying in bed. ______

The lawn mower was making a terrible noyse. ______

I was cheering so much that I lost my voyce. ______

We took the elevator from the foier to level three. ______

Sebastian is a very loial friend to me. ______

Challenge words

5 Write the word.

anoint ______

employ ______

choice ______

appoint ______

destroy ______

poise ______

oyster ______

voyage ______

poison ______

corduroy ______

6 Word clues. Which challenge word matches?

to apply oil as part of a religious ceremony ______

a long journey by land, air or sea ______

a substance that can harm or kill ______

to assign a job, role or position ______

fabric, typically used for pants ______

a sea animal that lives in a shell ______

7 Another way to say it. Which challenge word could replace the underlined word?

It was my <u>decision</u> to stay at home. ______

The superhero was trying to <u>smash</u> the evil villain. ______

Dad had to <u>hire</u> a plumber to fix the pipes. ______

The explorers are planning a <u>journey</u> around the world. ______

Our teacher is going to <u>nominate</u> a new class helper. ______

Words with the ch sound

List **1 Write the word.**

itch ______
patch ______
catch ______
ditch ______
fetch ______
bench ______
munch ______
match ______
witch ______
pinch ______
clutch ______
snatch ______
stitch ______
twitch ______
sketch ______
ranch ______
branch ______
switch ______
scratch ______
watch ______

2 *ch* words

______ ______
______ ______
______ ______

***tch* words**

______ ______
______ ______
______ ______
______ ______
______ ______
______ ______
______ ______
______ ______

3 In a group. Write the list word that belongs in each group.

seat, chair, ______
draw, paint, ______
clock, timer, ______
stick, leaf, ______
chew, crunch, ______
land, farm, ______

4 Name.

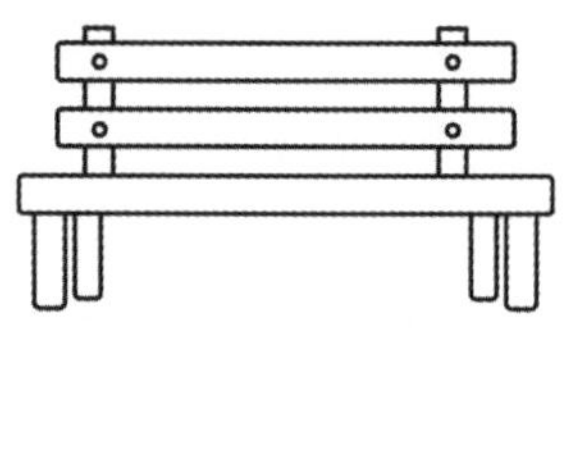
______

______

______

______

Words with the ch sound

5 Underline the spelling mistake. Write the word correctly.

I had an ietch I couldn't scratch. ______

We sat on the greenest petch of grass. ______

I told my dog to fech the ball. ______

I like to muntch on a carrot when doing my homework. ______

He tried to snach the ball. ______

Mum had to stich the hole in my pants. ______

I tried to cach the glass before it fell. ______

He accidentally drove into a dich. ______

Someone turned off the light swich. ______

Our soccer team won their final maetch. ______

Challenge words

6 Write the word.

wretch ______

kitchen ______

blotchy ______

butcher ______

satchel ______

quench ______

launch ______

scrunch ______

stretch ______

hatchet ______

7 Complete the sentence.

Use a ______ to chop the firewood.

We buy our meat from the local ______.

The scientist counted down to the rocket ______.

I carry my books in a ______.

The rash made her skin all ______.

I like to ______ the autumn leaves under my feet.

You should ______ before sport.

We cook all our food in the ______.

Being kept inside all day made her such a miserable ______.

8 Word clues. Which challenge word matches?

to satisfy one's thirst ______

someone who is very unhappy ______

a small bag ______

a small axe ______

Trigraphs – air and eer

List

fair
deer
hair
peer
veer
pair
jeer
hairy
airy
chair
repair
steer
dairy
sneer
cheer
fairy
stair
lair
flair
sheer

1 Write the word.

2 Fill in the missing letters.

re ___ ___ ir

pe ___ ___

j ___ ___ r

d ___ i ___ y

sn ___ ___ r

f ___ ___ ry

s ___ e ___ r

sta ___ r

3 Word clues. Which list word matches?

something you sit on ______________

it grows on your head ______________

two things that are alike ______________

to fix something ______________

shout of encouragement ______________

made from milk ______________

to move in a certain direction ______________

4 Name.

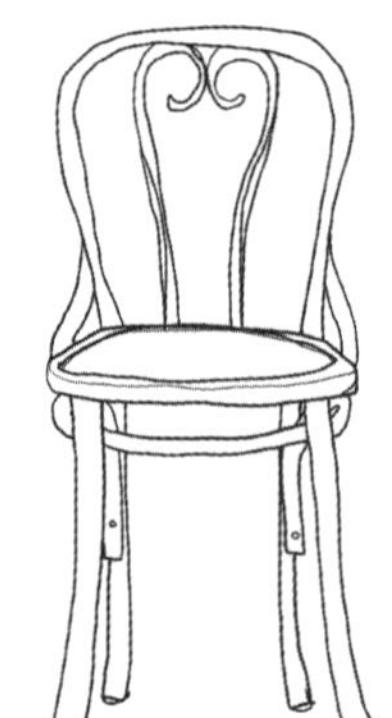

Trigraphs – air and eer

5 Underline the spelling mistakes. Write the word correctly.

The judge wanted to give him a feir trial. __________

The deir had two large antlers. __________

The fan beside me began to jeir the team. __________

That hole in the ground is a fox's leir. __________

The Captain had to steir the ship into the harbour. __________

The cows were raised on a deiry farm. __________

The giant spider in my room had eight long and heiry legs. __________

She has a fleir for dancing. __________

My brother almost tripped on the top steir. __________

A cheir went up from the crowd. __________

Challenge words

6 Write the word.

pioneer __________

mountaineer __________

staircase __________

eerie __________

engineer __________

volunteer __________

despair __________

career __________

fairly __________

mohair __________

7 Complete the sentence.

Ali wanted a __________ as a chef.

The __________ drew maps of the strange land.

Her jumper was made from __________.

We walked up the __________.

8 Hidden words. Find the challenge word.

ounmtamountaineerinterm __________

eeirieerieieirie __________

lyairffairlyiraf __________

ohmirmohairirhmo __________

oinpepioneeriopner __________

9 Word clues. Which challenge word matches?

one of the first people to do something __________

a mountain climber __________

weird and frightening __________

soft wool made from the fleece of a goat __________

Plurals – s, es

List **1 Write the word.**

bats ____________
foxes ____________
socks ____________
pianos ____________
birds ____________
buses ____________
dishes ____________
tomatoes ____________
mixes ____________
buzzes ____________
towers ____________
bushes ____________
skills ____________
mouths ____________
punches ____________
packets ____________
wishes ____________
silks ____________
echoes ____________
marches ____________

2 Complete the table.

Singular	Plural
sock	
bus	
wish	
bird	
	foxes
	mouths
packet	
	tomatoes
piano	
dish	

3 Unscramble these list words.

wersto	____________	oxsef	____________
unchpes	____________	matoesto	____________
anpios	____________	irbds	____________
archems	____________	zzbues	____________
ochese	____________	lksis	____________
ackpets	____________	outhms	____________

4 Name.

____

____

____

____

Plurals – s, es

5 In a group. Write the list word that belongs in each group.

shoes, laces, ______

feathers, nests, ______

carrots, onions, ______

keys, music, ______

balls, rackets, ______

trains, cars, ______

6 Fill in the missing letters.

mar __ __ es	__ __ zze __
p __ __ k __ t __	e __ __ o __ s
sk __ __ __ s	w __ __ h __ s
__ i __ e __	p __ n __ h __ s
f__ __ e __	__ ou __ __ __
t__ __ __t__ __ __	b __ __ e __
__ o __ er __	s __ __ __ s

Challenge words

7 Write the word.

peaches ______

crosses ______

sopranos ______

tattoos ______

churches ______

stretchers ______

coaches ______

houses ______

superheroes ______

slippers ______

8 Complete the sentence.

The school hired two ______ to take us on our excursion.

We bought a box of juicy ______ at the market.

I wear my ______ to keep my feet warm.

The pirate pointed to the ______ of sailing ships on his arms.

The ______ in the choir sing the high notes.

Spiderman and Batman are my favourite ______.

9 Word clues. Which challenge word matches?

fruit ______	characters with powers ______
warm shoes ______	places people live ______
places of worship ______	singers ______

10 Hidden words. Find the challenge word.

hhcoacoachescohce ______	ottostattoosattos ______
chtserstretchersthce ______	oushhouseshos ______
ssoesccrossesrross ______	

Silent letters – b, l, h

List

1 Write the word.

lamb ____
limb ____
walk ____
bomb ____
calf ____
talk ____
hour ____
numb ____
comb ____
palm ____
crumb ____
should ____
could ____
climb ____
thumb ____
yolk ____
tomb ____
chalk ____
honest ____
half ____

2 Sort the words.

Silent *b*	Silent *l*	Silent *h*

3 In a group. Write the list word that belongs in each group.

sheep, ram, ____
chat, conversation, ____
egg, shell, ____
true, genuine, ____
second, minute, ____
fingers, hand, ____

4 Name.

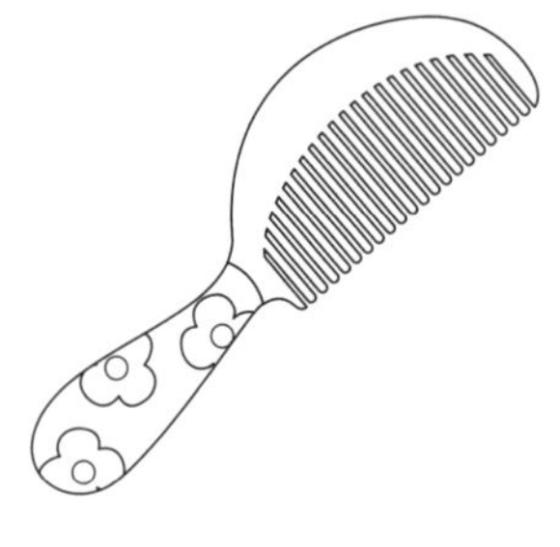
____

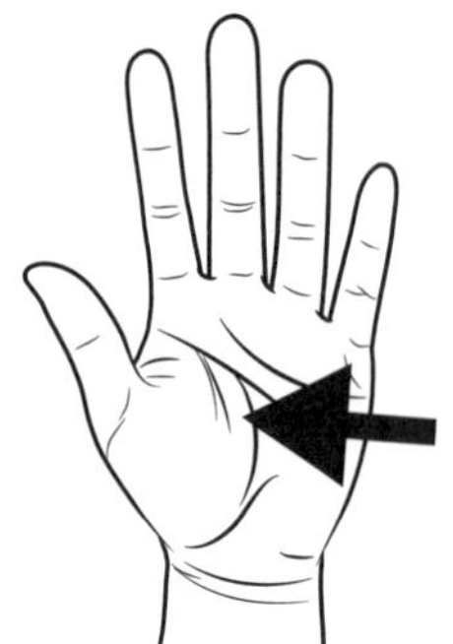
____

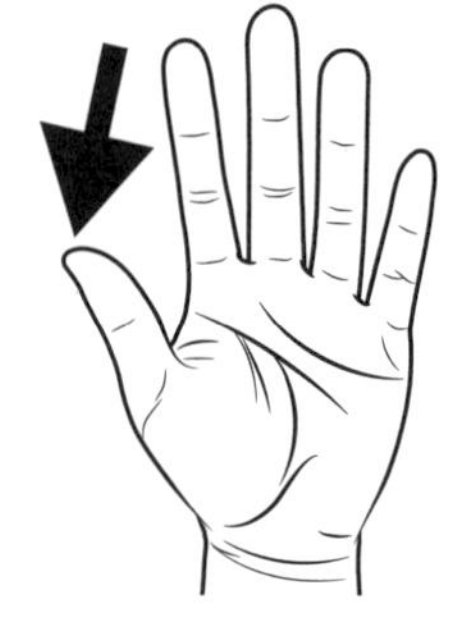
____

____

Silent letters – b, l, h

5 Underline the spelling mistakes. Write the word correctly.

I coud not believe I won the race! ____________

I shoud have finished my homework last night. ____________

The ancient pharaoh was buried in a golden tom. ____________

It's hard to com my curly hair. ____________

I felt num after swimming in the cold water. ____________

There is only an our of school left. ____________

We hung the swing from the lim of the tree. ____________

Not many classrooms have a blackboard and chauk. ____________

Challenge words

6 Write the word.

would ____________

exhaust ____________

folk ____________

heir ____________

plumber ____________

salmon ____________

debt ____________

doubt ____________

honour ____________

shepherd ____________

7 Complete the sentence.

The prince is the ____________ to the throne.

We hired a ____________ to fix our kitchen sink.

It is an ____________ to receive a medal.

Running may ____________ your energy.

The ____________ had a small flock of sheep.

They decided they ____________ order pizza.

I ____________ he has a pet tiger.

I paid off my ____________.

That story is just an old ____________ tale.

Dad went fishing and caught a huge ____________.

8 Word clues. Which challenge word matches?

fish ____________

broken pipe ____________

money ____________

sheep ____________

people ____________

9 Hidden words. Find the challenge word.

auseexhausthaust ____________

oidudsbtdodoubt ____________

onhonourhorueor ____________

ldowwouldllddw ____________

eeirheireerihie ____________

Suffixes – ing

List	1 Write the word.
mixing	______
eating	______
panting	______
asking	______
trying	______
lending	______
sleeping	______
washing	______
dreaming	______
painting	______
carrying	______
selling	______
falling	______
roaring	______
pouring	______
moving	______
hoping	______
baking	______
wiping	______
ruling	______

2 Complete the sentence with a list word.

To make money I am ______ my old bike.

Rain is ______ from the sky.

Nick was ______ the flour and eggs together.

Tina is ______ a picture of her dog.

She is ______ juice into her cup.

I was ______ Mum would make us pancakes, but she boiled eggs instead.

Dad is ______ a chocolate cake for my birthday.

The hungry lion began ______ for food.

3 Fill in the missing letters.

r __ a __ ing	le __ __ ing
__ ant __ __ g	__ __ eep __ __ g
as __ __ __ g	ca __ __ y __ __ g
tr __ __ ng	pai __ __ __ ng

4 Word building. Add suffixes to build words.

	ing	ed
paint		
pour		
roar		
dream		
ask		
bake		
wipe		
hope		

Suffixes – ing

5 Underline the spelling mistakes. Write the list word correctly.

The dog was pannting in the heat. ______

Tomorrow we are mooving from the country to the city. ______

It is difficult ruleing a margin without a ruler. ______

I am always lennding my books, but I never get them back. ______

I got excited when I heard the lion roarring. ______

My brother is always assking for more of everything. ______

We have to be quiet because my sister is sleping upstairs. ______

Challenge words

6 Write the word.

teasing ______

scaring ______

blaming ______

smiling ______

snoring ______

crossing ______

spraying ______

praising ______

freezing ______

whining ______

7 Complete the sentence.

The ghost story was s______ the children.

Miles is always b______ others for his mistakes.

Dad was s______ like a tractor.

We look both ways before c______ the road.

Max got in trouble for t______ his sister.

It was f______ cold outside in winter.

8 Hidden words. Find the challenge word.

irpapraisingainpr ______

hwinwhininghwing ______

ryaspsprayingygns ______

msilssmilingsimln ______

ferzfreezingferze ______

ssingcrossingcorss ______

9 Another way to say it. Which challenge word could replace the underlined word?

The thunder was <u>frightening</u> the dog. ______

My cousin is always <u>complaining</u>. ______

When I won the race I couldn't stop <u>grinning</u>. ______

Vowel trigraph – igh

List **1. Write the word.**

high ____
sigh ____
nigh ____
fight ____
night ____
right ____
sight ____
tight ____
might ____
light ____
alight ____
thigh ____
mighty ____
flight ____
slight ____
bright ____
delight ____
alright ____
fright ____
knight ____

2 Word clues. Which list word matches?

a medieval soldier ____
great happiness or joy ____
the action of flying ____
fear or terror ____
the ability to see ____
between your hip and knee ____

3 Opposites. Find the opposites.

low ____
day ____
left ____
loose ____
dark ____
dim ____

4 Unscramble the words.

ghribt ____
sghi ____
ghfit ____
nghi ____
ghitn ____
ghtri ____
ghsit ____
ghtit ____

5 Missing letters. Fill in the missing letters.

m ___ ___ h ___ ___
de ___ ___ ___ ___ ___
a ___ ri ___ ___ t
sl ___ ___ ___ t
f ___ i ___ ___ t
n ___ ___ ___ t
a ___ ___ ___ ht
kn ___ ___ ___ ___

Vowel trigraph – igh

3.10

6 Underline the spelling mistakes. Write the word correctly.

The bird sat hii in the tree. ________

We always phight over the remote. ________

Do we turn left or ryht? ________

The sky was alyte with fireworks. ________

We heard a myghty roar from the waterfall. ________

It mite rain today. ________

The time to leave is nie. ________

He gave a shigh of relief. ________

Challenge words

7 Write the word.

height ________

eyesight ________

firelight ________

insight ________

frighten ________

midnight ________

copyright ________

plight ________

fortnight ________

righteous ________

8 Word clues. Which challenge word matches?

light cast from a fire ________

twelve o'clock at night ________

two weeks ________

ability to see ________

how tall ________

to scare ________

morally right ________

an unhappy situation ________

protection of one's work ________

understanding something ________

9 Complete the sentence.

Her ________ is 165 cm.

A ________ is 14 days.

You need glasses if you have poor ________.

The author protected her work with ________.

The clock chimed 12 times at ________.

Suffixes – ing with short vowels

List **1 Write the word.**

batting ______________
fitting ______________
hopping ______________
getting ______________
winning ______________
rotting ______________
running ______________
tapping ______________
fanning ______________
sitting ______________
clapping ______________
shutting ______________
dropping ______________
slipping ______________
dripping ______________
shopping ______________
chatting ______________
tripping ______________
grabbing ______________
swimming ______________

2 Unscramble these list words.

ttbaing ______________
ppingtri ______________
bbgraing ______________
sliingpp ______________
ingfitt ______________
nnniigw ______________

3 Opposites. Find the opposite.

losing ______________
opening ______________
standing ______________
giving ______________
walking ______________

4 Missing letters. Write the missing letters.

___ op ___ ___ ___ ___
r ___ ___ ni ___ g
___ rop ___ ___ ___ g
ch ___ ___ tin ___
dri ___ ___ i ___ g

5 Underline the spelling mistakes. Write the word correctly.

The children are runing around the oval. ______________
The sound of the driping tap kept me up all night. ______________
I'm sure I heard someone tappping on the window. ______________
I found the cat siting on the windowsill. ______________
People are always slypping over on the wet tiles. ______________
The apples are roting in the orchard. ______________
They were wining as they had the most points. ______________

Suffixes – ing with short vowels

6 Complete each sentence with a list word.

The children are ________________ twenty laps of the pool.

She is ________________ a new kitten.

It's so hot, I am ________________ myself with my book.

The apple was so old it was ________________ .

We could hear the crowd ________________ and cheering.

Right on the buzzer, Jono scored the ________________ goal.

We went ________________ for some new winter clothes.

She keeps ________________ over her own feet.

Challenge words

7 Write the word.

splitting ________________

wrapping ________________

scrapping ________________

beginning ________________

programming ________________

permitting ________________

forbidding ________________

submitting ________________

squatting ________________

regretting ________________

8 Hidden words. Find the challenge word.

bidfoforbiddingfidbg ________________

bsmitsubmittingsngus ________________

suqtsisquattingttisu ________________

crsapscrappingcrps ________________

raprwrappingwrpi ________________

KEEP OUT

9 Complete the sentence.

He is ________________ wood for the fire.

My brother is ________________ our computer to block viruses.

She is ________________ not bringing her jumper on such a cold day.

The school is finally ________________ students to use the new playground.

January is the ________________ of the new year.

The girls were ________________ the presents in paper.

Words with the same end sound – ei, ey and eigh 3.12

List **1 Write the word.**

List	
reins	
prey	
vein	
veil	
eight	
grey	
they	
obey	
weigh	
neigh	
weighed	
beige	
eighth	
sleigh	
obeyed	
obeying	
weighing	
eighty	
eighteen	
eighteenth	

2 Sort the words.

ei	*ey*	*eigh*

3 Word clues. Which list word matches?

two less than twenty ______
the sound a horse makes ______
worn over the face ______
one more than seven ______
following a command ______
pale brown colour ______
transports blood ______

4 Meaning. Which list word means?

leather straps attached to a horse's bridle ______
an animal that is hunted by another ______
to measure using a scale ______
a cart used to transport people over snow ______
vessel that carries blood towards the heart ______
to carry out a command or instruction ______
thin cloth worn over the head and shoulders ______
the number after 7 and before 9 ______

8

Words with the same end sound – ei, ey and eigh 3.12

5 Underline the spelling mistake. Write the word correctly.

One less that nineteen is eyteen. __________

Her pants were a boring beighe colour. __________

We are weying things in the kitchen to find the heaviest. __________

I've already read seven of her books; I'm now on the eyghth. __________

The school rules must be obeighed. __________

My grandfather is eity years old. __________

The largest veighn in our body is connected to our heart. __________

It's important to obeigh traffic signs. __________

Challenge words

6 Write the word.

- convey __________
- survey __________
- neighing __________
- freighter __________
- neighbour __________
- feint __________
- neighbourly __________
- freight __________
- lightweight __________
- weightlifter __________

7 Word clues. Which challenge word matches?

to collect specific information __________

a ship that transports goods __________

a person that lives close to you __________

a false movement __________

a person who lifts heavy items competitively __________

noise a horse makes __________

8 Complete the sentence.

Playing loud music late at night is not very __________.

The horses were __________ loudly.

I will __________ the news to them.

I wasn't fooled by his __________ to the right.

__________ is moved by land, sea and air.

We tallied the __________ data.

I'll bring a __________ jacket because the weather is still warm.

Word endings – le, el, al

List 1 Write the word.

little ______
table ______
uncle ______
angel ______
apple ______
royal ______
candle ______
bottle ______
camel ______
final ______
purple ______
temple ______
gentle ______
normal ______
cattle ______
bundle ______
travel ______
local ______
people ______
equal ______

2 Sort the words.

le	*el*	*al*

3 In a group. Write the list word that belongs in each group.

tiny, small, ______

journey, holiday, ______

pear, orange, ______

aunty, cousin, ______

sheep, horses, ______

average, standard, ______

king, queen, ______

wax, flame, ______

4 Name.

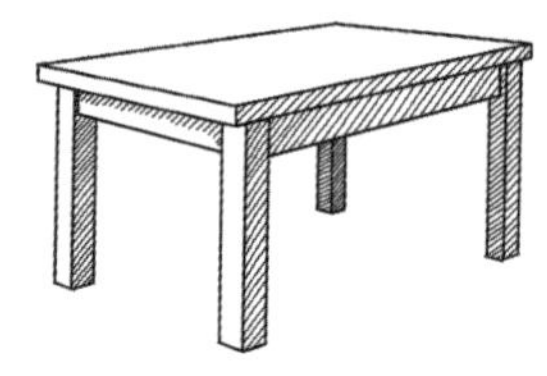

Word endings – le, el, al

5 Meaning. Which list word means?

to have the same value or amount as something else ______

a place of worship ______

a stick of wax burned to give light ______

large animal used for crossing deserts ______

a piece of furniture with a flat top ______

used to hold liquid ______

a parent's brother ______

a human figure with wings ______

Challenge words

6 Write the word.

marvel ______

parcel ______

example ______

floral ______

trouble ______

couple ______

channel ______

tribal ______

struggle ______

vehicle ______

7 Complete the sentence.

I received a ______ in the mail.

A daffodil is an ______ of a flower.

My brother got into ______ for staying up late.

I wanted to change the ______ but couldn't find the remote!

It was a ______ to get my new bed upstairs.

A car is an example of a ______ .

She has a ______ pattern on her shorts.

8 Word clues. Which challenge word matches?

flower pattern ______

transport ______

hard ______

wonder ______

model to be copied ______

two ______

package ______

Suffixes – ed

List

1 Write the word.

asked ______
cooked ______
mixed ______
yelled ______
dusted ______
cared ______
liked ______
tamed ______
hoped ______
loved ______
washed ______
kicked ______
roared ______
smiled ______
stared ______
pleased ______
spilled ______
warmed ______
roasted ______
poured ______

2 Unscramble the words.

ovdle ______ heasdw ______
mrawed ______ usdted ______
staoedr ______ milsed ______
dekcik ______ arestd ______

3 Missing letter. Write the missing letter.

y __ __ led
pl __ __ __ ed
__ __ ured
m __ __ __ d
__ oo __ __ __
a __ __ __ d
r __ __ __ ed
__ __ ill __ __

4 Chunks. Rearrange the chunks to make a list word.

ed ar m w ______
sh ed wa ______
ed k k ic ______
as ed le p ______
ill ed sp ______
as ted ro ______

5 Complete the table.

smile	
	liked
dust	
yell	
	cooked
	washed
love	
mix	

Suffixes – ed

6 Underline the spelling mistakes. Write the word correctly.

My teacher was plesed with my progress. ____________

The station workers taimed the wild horses. ____________

We rosted marshmallows around the campfire. ____________

The heater warmd our freezing hands and feet. ____________

Mum got angry when I spillid hot chocolate on the carpet. ____________

Dad cooced so much, so that we still have leftovers. ____________

I kiked the ball so high, it landed on the roof! ____________

Challenge words

7 Write the word.

enjoyed ____________

praised ____________

visited ____________

wheeled ____________

ordered ____________

admired ____________

appeared ____________

breathed ____________

frightened ____________

remembered ____________

8 Complete the sentence.

Sam e____________ his visit to the zoo.

I v____________ my grandparents.

Mum o____________ silence!

I r____________ to pack my overdue library books.

Dad p____________ us for our quick thinking.

I a____________ him for his bravery.

He a____________ out of nowhere.

I w____________ the trolley down the supermarket aisles.

9 Hidden words. Find the challenge word hidden in these letters.

earpeappearedppere ____________

eatbrbreathedklp ____________

ghtefrfrightenedefri ____________

welwheeledhwehel ____________

joyenjoyedenjo ____________

arisepraisedprai ____________

rredoordereddde ____________

emebrememberededed ____________

mireadmiredded ____________

ttdevisitedvssit ____________

Homophones

List 1 Write the word.

mane ______
main ______
meat ______
meet ______
plane ______
plain ______
for ______
four ______
by ______
buy ______
not ______
knot ______
seen ______
scene ______
great ______
grate ______
groan ______
grown ______
who's ______
whose ______

2 In a group. Write the list word that belongs in each group.

tail, claw, ______
car, boat, ______
moan, cry, ______
fantastic, wonderful, ______
two, three, ______
rope, string, ______
bought, purchase, ______

3 Word clues. Which list word matches?

no decoration ______
very good ______
the most important ______
the number after three ______
place an event happens ______
produce sold by a butcher ______
a grunt or deep sound ______
next to or near ______
to have looked at ______
who is ______

4 Name.

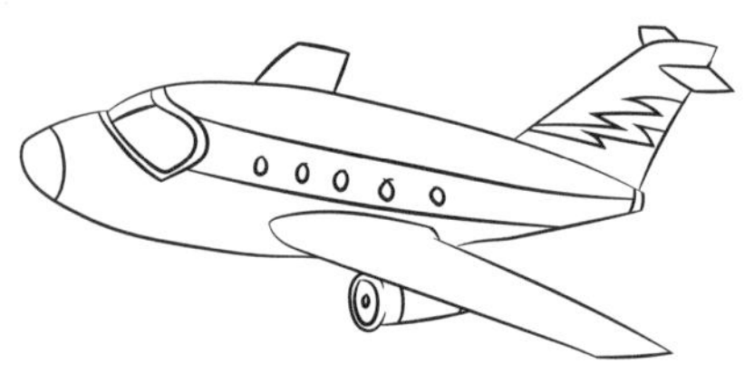

4

______ ______ ______ ______

Homophones

5 Underline the spelling mistake. Write the word correctly.

The lion had a big, bushy main. ______________

Who's schoolbag is at the door? ______________

The recipe says to great two whole carrots. ______________

I didn't have money to by an ice-cream. ______________

My younger sister is for years old. ______________

Have you scene the latest episode? ______________

We agreed to meat after school. ______________

The passengers started to board the plain. ______________

Challenge words

6 Write the word.

herd ______________

heard ______________

berry ______________

bury ______________

heel ______________

heal ______________

he'll ______________

rain ______________

rein ______________

reign ______________

7 Word clues. Which challenge word matches?

group of animals ______________

a small juicy fruit ______________

water from the sky ______________

leather strap ______________

part of your foot ______________

make healthy again ______________

8 Complete the sentence.

I ______________ a loud noise and went to investigate.

The weather forecast predicted heavy ______________.

The dog likes to ______________ bones in the backyard.

The ______________ of cows grazed quietly in the paddock.

The Queen had a long and prosperous ______________.

I had a cut on the ______________ of my foot.

Silent letters – k, g, w

List **1 Write the word.**

knee ______
knit ______
knot ______
know ______
sign ______
knight ______
reign ______
sword ______
write ______
knock ______
knife ______
knead ______
knack ______
gnat ______
wren ______
design ______
gnome ______
gnash ______
wreck ______
wrong ______

2 Sort the words.

silent *k*	silent *g*	silent *w*

3 Name.

______ ______

______

4 Word clues. Which list word matches?

a weapon with a long pointed blade ______
a small fairytale creature ______
a joint in a leg ______
a small insect with two wings ______
a king or queen's time of ruling ______
a small bird ______
to tap or hit something ______
a natural talent or ability ______
to grind your teeth together ______

Silent letters – k, g, w

5 Underline the spelling mistake. Write the word correctly.

In class we were asked to desin a new form of transport. ______________

The divers approached the old reck. ______________

I eat dinner with a nife and fork. ______________

You must nead the dough before baking it in the oven. ______________

I rite in my journal every night. ______________

I couldn't see the street sin, so we missed the turn-off. ______________

My mum is teaching me how to nit my own scarf. ______________

The night wore protective armour. ______________

Challenge words

6 Write the word.

knuckle ______________

knapsack ______________

gnarl ______________

wrestle ______________

knowledge ______________

written ______________

foreign ______________

wrought ______________

wreckage ______________

playwright ______________

7 Word clues. Which challenge word matches?

a knot or bulge ______________

one who writes plays ______________

the joint in a finger ______________

a bag ______________

to struggle or fight ______________

from another country ______________

8 Complete the sentence.

Mia couldn't get the ring over her ______________.

I packed my school books into my ______________.

There is a lot of ______________ collected in a library.

She had ______________ a good report.

The ______________ was scattered everywhere after the natural disaster.

The ______________ received excellent reviews for his latest production.

There was a ______________ on the trunk of the tree.

Suffixes – er, or

List

1 Write the word.

teacher ____________
worker ____________
seller ____________
singer ____________
swimmer ____________
runner ____________
driver ____________
baker ____________
collector ____________
jogger ____________
painter ____________
gardener ____________
climber ____________
printer ____________
editor ____________
wrapper ____________
director ____________
conductor ____________
supporter ____________
builder ____________

2 Sort the words.

er	*or*

3 In a group. Write the list word that belongs in each group.

school, classroom, ____________
microphone, music, ____________
brushes, canvas, ____________
flour, bread, ____________
tools, bricks, ____________
pool, laps, ____________
plants, seeds, ____________
running, exercise, ____________
actor, set, ____________

4 Chunks. Rearrange the syllables to make a list word.

tor-lec-col ____________
duc-tor-con ____________
por-sup-ter ____________
ber-clim ____________
ain-p-ter ____________
ell-er-s ____________

Suffixes – er, or

5 Underline the spelling mistakes. Write the word correctly.

The directer won an award for her latest film. ______

I bought the book because it was a best sellor. ______

My dad is a collecter of toy cars and old coins. ______

The runnor was training hard for the marathon. ______

His dream is to become the conducter of a world famous orchestra. ______

The truck drivor has to be careful of smaller cars and vehicles on the road. ______

Challenge words

6 Write the word.

commander ______
manager ______
educator ______
attacker ______
knitter ______
decorator ______
elevator ______
exhibitor ______
navigator ______
foreigner ______

7 Complete the sentence.

My teacher is an ______.

The store ______ gave us a discount.

The ______ directed the ship.

The ______ painted the room blue.

The ______ made the longest scarf.

The ______ felt nervous in his new country.

We took the ______ to the top floor.

8 Hidden words. Find the challenge word hidden in these letters.

ckerattackerattkl ______
mdercommanderandc ______
ibitorexhibitorexhiv ______
angermanagermanage ______
torceducatorduee ______
atorlelevatorele ______
ratordecoratorceod ______
rkkktknitterqlps ______
erfpforeignerfor ______
togatnavigatoravi ______

Consonant digraphs – wh, ph, gh

List **1 Write the word.**

why ____________
what ____________
when ____________
phone ____________
ghost ____________
white ____________
which ____________
while ____________
graph ____________
photo ____________
whip ____________
whale ____________
where ____________
phase ____________
gherkin ____________
wheat ____________
whisper ____________
wheel ____________
whimper ____________
whirl ____________

2 Word clues. Which list word matches?

camera ____________
data ____________
scary ____________
call ____________
ocean ____________
flour ____________
pickle ____________
quiet ____________

3 Complete each sentence with a list word.

I heard the ____________ ringing, but no-one would answer it.

A blue ____________ is the largest animal on Earth.

I always pick the ____________ out of my burger.

I took a ____________ of my cat with mum's new camera.

The back ____________ on my new bike is bent.

The ____________ fluffy cloud looked like a dinosaur in the sky.

Our teacher made a ____________ to show the results from our survey.

I couldn't decide ____________ pair of shoes I wanted to wear.

4 Name.

____________ ____________ ____________ ____________

Consonant digraphs – wh, ph, gh

5 Sort the words.

wh		*ph*	*gh*

Challenge words

6 Write the word.

whinge ________________
whelp ________________
pharaoh ________________
physical ________________
wharf ________________
whether ________________
wheeze ________________
photograph ________________
ghoul ________________
ghastly ________________

7 Hidden words. Find the challenge word.

phyisphysicalciphy ________________
thewewhetherthewr ________________
eewhewheezeezewe ________________
asthyghastlyghats ________________
arfwhwharfarfhw ________________
gahrpphotographggh ________________
lpwwhelpelpy ________________
aroahpharaoharah ________________
oughghoulool ________________
lghaghastlygrsp ________________

8 Word clues. Which challenge word matches?

king of Ancient Egypt ________________
to constantly complain ________________
where ships and boats dock ________________
an evil spirit ________________
a picture made by a camera ________________
the newborn of certain mammals ________________

Suffixes – ies, ied

List

1 Write the word.

tried ______
flies ______
cried ______
spies ______
fried ______
dries ______
copies ______
tidied ______
studied ______
carries ______
fancies ______
worried ______
bullies ______
married ______
denies ______
hurried ______
buries ______
partied ______
relied ______
empties ______

2 Sort the words.

ies words

______ ______
______ ______
______ ______
______ ______
______ ______
______ ______

ied words

______ ______
______ ______
______ ______
______ ______
______ ______

3 Complete each sentence with a list word.

I ______ the mess in my room.

I was ______ I had left something behind.

The little girl always ______ her teddy bear around with her.

I ______ hard for my test and passed with flying colours.

He ______ out the door so he wouldn't miss his bus.

My uncle and aunt have been ______ to each other for years.

4 Chunks. Rearrange the letters to make a list word.

ie s sp ______
ll s bu ie ______
pa ied rt ______
d fr ie ______
pt ies em ______
u die d st ______

Suffixes – ies, ied

5 Meaning. Which list word means?

attempted ______
likes or attracted to ______
refuses to agree with ______
to have trusted or depended on ______
moves through the air using wings ______
to have shed tears ______

Challenge words

6 Write the word.

supplies ______
replied ______
queries ______
applies ______
qualifies ______
purified ______
remedied ______
occupies ______
satisfied ______
identified ______

7 Hidden words. Find the challenge word.

yheequalifiestoqu ______
syusatisfiedbusj ______
uyadappliesbhai ______
xualoccupiesbyua ______
pouenpurifiedupaq ______
stamsupplieskgiuu ______
eyidentifiedoiyn ______
aserepliedkjbu ______
opihremedieduoya ______
apqueriesqrsl ______

8 Another way to say it. Which challenge word could replace the underlined word?

The medicine cured his headache. ______
The company provides food for homeless people. ______
The bird watcher recognised the bird. ______
Tony responded to the email. ______
Sarah questions whether to go to the party. ______
The armchair fills a corner of the room. ______
The team had fulfilled all of the requirements to qualify. ______
Toby passes for his drivers licence because he passed the test. ______

Spelling patterns – augh, ough

List

1 Write the word.

laugh ______
ought ______
bought ______
caught ______
fought ______
taught ______
though ______
brought ______
thought ______
through ______
naughty ______
cough ______
enough ______
rough ______
laughter ______
dough ______
tough ______
plough ______
daughter ______
drought ______

2 Complete the word with *augh* or *ough*.

l______ d______

th______t t______t

3 In a group. Write the list word that belongs in each group.

bring, bringing, ______
catch, catching, ______
laugh, laughing, ______
think, thinking, ______
teach, teaching, ______
buy, buying, ______

4 Meaning. Which list word means?

in one end and out the other ______
flour and water that is baked into bread ______
to have purchased an item ______
to force air noisily from the lungs ______
a person's female child ______
uneven or bumpy ______
a long period without rain ______
did battle or took part in a struggle ______

Spelling patterns – augh, ough

5 Underline the spelling mistake. Write the word correctly.

Two strong horses pulled the plaugh through the fields. __________

The police cought the thieves red-handed. __________

My mother is my grandfather's doughter. __________

Micky was very noughty to put paint all over the walls. __________

Sue had a nasty caugh when she was sick. __________

Amy thaught that lunchtime was too short. __________

We mixed flour and water to make daugh. __________

Nate braught his best drawings to school. __________

There was not enaugh food to go around. __________

I had to lough at my brother's impression of a pigeon. __________

Challenge words

6 Write the word.

bough __________

draught __________

sought __________

throughout __________

thorough __________

trough __________

wrought __________

haughty __________

onslaught __________

distraught __________

7 Complete the sentence.

The pig ate at the __________.

We searched __________ the whole house but couldn't find the ball.

They hung a swing from a __________ on the tree.

They __________ advice from their parents.

The __________ iron gate slammed shut behind them.

The cleaners did a __________ clean of the whole house.

8 Word clues. Which challenge word matches?

a current of air in a room __________

anxiously worried __________

a forceful, sudden attack __________

thinking that others are not as good as __________

to have looked for something __________

Suffixes ed – with short vowels

List

batted
fanned
tapped
ripped
hopped
petted
jutted
rotted
sobbed
hummed
slipped
shopped
chipped
drummed
snapped
wrapped
grinned
dragged
spotted
slammed

1 Write the word.

batted ______
fanned ______
tapped ______
ripped ______
hopped ______
petted ______
jutted ______
rotted ______
sobbed ______
hummed ______
slipped ______
shopped ______
chipped ______
drummed ______
snapped ______
wrapped ______
grinned ______
dragged ______
spotted ______
slammed ______

2 Double the last letter then add *ed*.

tap ______
wrap ______
drum ______
hop ______
jut ______
snap ______
slip ______
sob ______
drag ______
slam ______

3 In a group. Write the list word that belongs in each group.

knocked, rapped, ______
cloaked, enveloped, ______
shut, banged, ______
slid, tripped, ______
stained, decayed, ______
blew, cooled, ______

4 Meaning. Which list word means?

stuck out sharply ______
patted or stroked an animal ______
hit a ball ______
made a singing sound without opening the lips ______
smiled broadly ______
broke a small piece of something ______
decomposed or decayed ______
shut with force and a loud noise ______

Suffixes ed – with short vowels

5 Fill in the missing word.

I ______________ a hole in my pants when I jumped over the fence.

The frog ______________ around the edge of the pond before diving in.

The edge of the tea cup was ______________ after I dropped it.

We ______________ all day, but I still didn't find a dress for the party.

I put my arms around her and hugged her as she ______________.

I ______________ a rhythm on my bongo drums.

I ______________ twigs in half so we could put them on the fire.

When she ______________ it made everyone feel happy.

We couldn't lift it, so we ______________ it across the floor.

On the way to school I ______________ a five dollar note on the ground.

Challenge words

6 Write the word.

stripped ______________

admitted ______________

scrapped ______________

permitted ______________

equipped ______________

shredded ______________

transmitted ______________

programmed ______________

embedded ______________

acquitted ______________

7 Complete the sentence.

He ______________ to eating the whole cake.

She was ______________ and ready to go camping.

Mum ______________ the sheets off the bed.

My brother ______________ his computer to wake him up each morning.

Dad ______________ me to stay at my friend's house.

The thorn was ______________ in his foot.

The man was ______________ of the crime.

8 Another way to say it. Which challenge word could replace the underlined word.

They <u>discarded</u> their original idea and started again. ______________

The man was <u>found not guilty</u> of the charge of theft. ______________

The TV show was <u>broadcast</u> from a small studio. ______________

My brother <u>tore</u> the lettuce for the tacos. ______________

They were <u>allowed</u> to attend the party if they cleaned up. ______________

Soft c and g

List **1 Write the word.**

gym ______
city ______
circus ______
giant ______
pencil ______
rice ______
magic ______
stage ______
huge ______
danger ______
orange ______
dance ______
village ______
engine ______
giraffe ______
grace ______
cycle ______
circle ______
angel ______
since ______

2 Unscramble these list words.

lilvgae ______
grnaoe ______
gffriae ______
cclye ______
angerd ______
necilp ______
gneal ______
rgcea ______

3 Sort the words.

soft c

______ ______
______ ______
______ ______
______ ______
______ ______

soft g

______ ______
______ ______
______ ______
______ ______
______ ______
______ ______

4 Name.

g______

c______

c______

Soft c and g

5 Word clues. Find the list word that fits.

a place people visit to get fit and healthy ______________

used to power a car ______________

performed by a magician ______________

a taller than normal human ______________

a platform used for performances ______________

something that could cause harm ______________

a small town ______________

a human figure with wings and a halo ______________

Challenge words

6 Write the word.

sentence ______________

lettuce ______________

intelligence ______________

embrace ______________

image ______________

general ______________

citizen ______________

garbage ______________

emergency ______________

cylinder ______________

7 Hidden words. Find the challenge word.

euixintelligenceuegyf ______________

golsdcitizensfosr ______________

sdfsentencebsowj ______________

lomagarbageyeln ______________

sabemergencyishk ______________

pltsimagehiklao ______________

8 Word clues. Which challenge word matches?

rubbish ______________

a vegetable ______________

a 3D shape ______________

9 Complete the sentence.

One of his chores is to take out the ______________.

A ______________ begins with a capital letter and ends with a full stop.

They called the ambulance as it was an ______________.

He chopped the ______________ for the salad.

The scientist is a person of great ______________.

Ranjit was a ______________ of two countries.

Irregular verbs – past tense

List **1 Write the word.**

broke ____
blew ____
told ____
slept ____
shook ____
began ____
became ____
chose ____
wrote ____
found ____
froze ____
knew ____
heard ____
awoke ____
burnt ____
slung ____
meant ____
struck ____
learnt ____
mistook ____

2 Chunks. Rearrange the letters to make a list word.

se ho c ____
nt r bu ____
ar he d ____
oo sh k ____
ew bl ____
ew kn ____
ea m nt ____
ck st ru ____

3 In a group. Write the list word that belongs in each group.

sleep, sleeping, ____
know, knowing, ____
strike, striking, ____
learn, learning, ____
find, finding, ____
begin, begun, ____
choose, choosing, ____
break, breaking, ____

4 Meaning. Which list word means?

started something ____
understood incorrectly ____
discovered something ____
received sound through the ears ____
sent out air from the mouth ____
picked one or more from a group ____
hardened into ice ____

Irregular verbs – past tense

5 Write the past tense of the word in brackets.

I (awake) ________________ early this morning.
Yesterday I (hear) ________________ that the weather will turn cold.
Last week I (break) ________________ Mum's flower pot.
She has already (tell) ________________ me the truth.
Last night I (sleep) ________________ for only four hours.
I (begin) ________________ my assignment last week.
The girl (become) ________________ sick after eating bad food.
I (write) ________________ him a long email to explain my decision.

Challenge words

6 Write the word.

shone ________________
knelt ________________
dealt ________________
built ________________
spread ________________
forgave ________________
understood ________________
withdrew ________________
forbade ________________
broadcast ________________

7 Hidden words. Find the challenge word.

asdugforgaveuoasghw ________________
suiabroadcastawoih ________________
sihslungusyk ________________
asyigforbadeough ________________
asuokneltushap ________________
asojdunderstoodiusa ________________

8 Word clues. Which challenge word matches?

produced light ________________
made or created ________________
prohibited ________________

9 Another way to say it. Which challenge word could replace the underlined word?

Mum <u>created</u> the cubbyhouse in just two days. ________________
The doctor <u>disallowed</u> Jade to play sport with her broken thumb. ________________
Shouting in the playground will <u>transmit</u> the news to everyone. ________________
The moon <u>glowed</u> in the dark night sky. ________________
They <u>excused</u> his bad behaviour as he was tired. ________________
The bird <u>lifted</u> its wings and flew away. ________________

Word endings – ary, ery and ory

List **1 Write the word.**

bakery ______
cookery ______
diary ______
bravery ______
factory ______
greenery ______
salary ______
misery ______
grocery ______
victory ______
battery ______
burglary ______
memory ______
mystery ______
delivery ______
library ______
nursery ______
summary ______
crockery ______
glossary ______

2 Sort the words.

ary words

______ ______
______ ______
______ ______
______ ______
______ ______
______ ______

ery words

______ ______
______ ______
______ ______
______ ______
______ ______
______ ______

ory words

______ ______
______ ______
______ ______
______ ______
______ ______
______ ______

3 Complete the word with *ery*, *ory* or *ary*.

batt______ gloss______
mis______ crock______
green______ summ______
cook______ groc______
burgl______ bak______

Word endings – ary, ery and ory

4 Match the word to the clue.

a book in which you write your thoughts and feelings d ____________

a building where items are produced f ____________

a set amount of money paid regularly for work s ____________

a win v ____________

the ability to remember m ____________

something that cannot be explained m ____________

a place where you can go to read and borrow books l ____________

a room for babies or young children n ____________

Challenge words

5 Write the word.

ordinary ____________

discovery ____________

territory ____________

upholstery ____________

vocabulary ____________

imaginary ____________

category ____________

dictionary ____________

laboratory ____________

necessary ____________

6 Analogy. Complete the analogy with a challenge word.

Front is to back as hiding is to ____________

Flat is to round as unimportant is to ____________

Black is to white as irregular is to ____________

On is to off as real is to ____________

House is to home as book is to ____________

Circle is to round as section is to ____________

7 Another way to say it. Which challenge word could replace the underlined word?

They moved from one <u>district</u> to another. ____________

We bought a gift even though it wasn't <u>needed</u>. ____________

She studied Japanese <u>language</u> for years. ____________

The unicorn is a <u>make-believe</u> horse with a horn. ____________

Wednesday was a completely <u>normal</u> day this week. ____________

This year I will be running in the U9 <u>section</u>. ____________

Suffixes – ful and less

List

painful
endless
helpful
restless
useful
homeless
thankful
careless
hopeful
harmless
beautiful
thoughtful
blameless
forgetful
truthful
fearless
powerful
awful
tasteless
skilful

1 Write the word.

2 Sort the words.

ful	*less*

3 Meaning. Which list word means?

not able to relax ______
having or using force ______
causing pain ______
very bad or terrible ______

4 Underline the spelling mistake. Write the word correctly.

During the long drive I was very restles and couldn't sit still. ______
The Internet is a usefull tool for researching assignments. ______
We found a homeles dog and took it to the animal shelter. ______
The careles driver ran a red light because he wasn't looking. ______
Henry is a truthfull person, who never lies. ______
The firefighter was fearles as he ran into a burning building. ______
The leftover food had an awfull smell. ______
He is a very skilfull player. ______
Mrs Potts planted some beautifull roses in her garden. ______

Suffixes – ful and less

5 Chunks. Rearrange the letters to make a list word.

ss ta le ste ______
in ful pa ______
ho ful pe ______
dl ss en e ______
lp ful he ______
le rm ss ha ______
a ful th nk ______
wer ful po ______

Challenge words

6 Write the word.

goalless ______
worthless ______
sorrowful ______
delightful ______
weightless ______
wonderful ______
successful ______
doubtful ______
respectful ______
pointless ______

7 Hidden words. Find the challenge word.

lodelightfuliohc ______
fulpointlesshsgbeu ______
hsirngoallessssuje ______
asidynweightlessahout ______
cksycworthlessuioet ______
aisudgsuccessfulaoh ______

8 Word clues. Which challenge word matches?

very sad ______
being polite ______
doing well ______
excellent or amazing ______
not likely or probable ______
without meaning ______

9 Another way to say it. Which challenge word could replace the underlined word?

Emma was always <u>considerate</u> of her parents' wishes. ______
He was a <u>prosperous</u> businessman who worked very hard. ______
The game ended in a <u>no-score</u> draw. ______
Chen was <u>uncertain</u> she would enjoy herself. ______
The whole thing seems <u>meaningless</u>. ______

Silent letters – t, n, u

List **1 Write the word.**

listen ____________
fasten ____________
castle ____________
often ____________
build ____________
guide ____________
rustle ____________
soften ____________
nestle ____________
guard ____________
biscuit ____________
bristle ____________
thistle ____________
glisten ____________
Christmas ____________
guess ____________
moisten ____________
guest ____________
autumn ____________
guitar ____________

2 Sort the words.

Silent *t*	Silent *n*	Silent *u*
____	____	____
____	____	____
____	____	____
____	____	____
____	____	____
____	____	____
____	____	____
____	____	____
____	____	____
____	____	____
____	____	____
____	____	____

3 Chunks. Rearrange the sections to make a list word.

st bri le ____________
ar gu it ____________
it bis cu ____________
mas Ch st ri ____________
le st ne ____________

4 Which silent letter is missing?

nes____le lis____en this____le g____ard bris____le
mois____en b____ild cas____le g____ide rus____le

5 Name.

____________ ____________ ____________

Silent letters – t, n, u

6 **Underline the spelling mistake.** Write the word correctly.

I always make sure I fasen my seatbelt. ______

Leaves turn brown in autum. ______

I can play three chords on the gitar. ______

I pricked my finger on a thisle. ______

Bright sunshine on the river makes it glissen. ______

I took a biscit from the jar. ______

In Paris we needed a gide to show us the sights. ______

The leaves rusle when the wind blows. ______

I have to lisen to my Dad's favourite music. ______

I tried to gess the number she was thinking of. ______

Challenge words

7 **Write the word.**

whistle ______

wrestle ______

hustle ______

column ______

trestle ______

disguise ______

guilty ______

circuit ______

hymn ______

guild ______

8 **Word clues.** Which challenge word matches?

responsible for doing something wrong ______

a structure that looks like a post ______

to hide someone's appearance ______

to make a shrill sound with your mouth ______

a song of praise ______

to move or work swiftly ______

9 **Complete the sentences.**

My little brothers would w______ all day if they were allowed.

The doctor visited every patient on her c______ of the town.

The t______ is the framework that holds up the bridge.

The screenwriters' g______ met monthly to make sure their rights were protected.

Compound words

List **1 Write the word.**

teaspoon ______
seafood ______
sunrise ______
toothbrush ______
baseball ______
rainbow ______
footprint ______
moonlight ______
eyesight ______
homework ______
shoelace ______
earring ______
grandmother ______
fireworks ______
waterfall ______
butterfly ______
sunflower ______
airport ______
keyhole ______
afternoon ______

2 Fill in the missing part.

tea______
moon______
tooth______
______fall
______ball
sun______
______bow
______noon
shoe______
sun______

3 Unscramble these words.

fsodeoa ______
oprnoftit ______
yseighte ______
eworhmko ______
wfirorkse ______
uttrefylb ______
irpatro ______
hyelkoe ______

4 Put the correct words together.

I like to go jogging in the afterwhere. ______
The recipe said to add a teaprint of sugar to the batter. ______
I watched a butterlight fly over the garden. ______
My grandstorm always makes the best lasagne. ______
How can I clean my teeth if I can't find my toothspoon? ______
We had fish and chips at a seaflower restaurant. ______
I wear glasses because my earsight is not very good. ______
We watched the fireboard explode in the sky. ______
Mum says if I don't finish my homeball, I can't watch TV. ______

Compound words

5 Write the compound word that these pictures make.

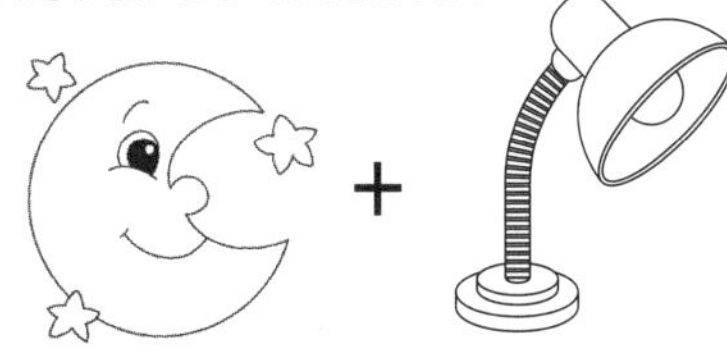

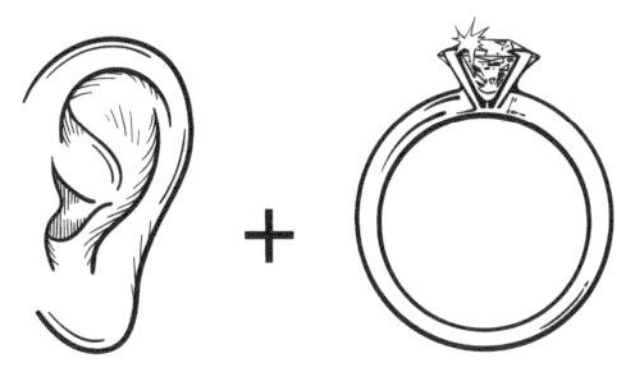

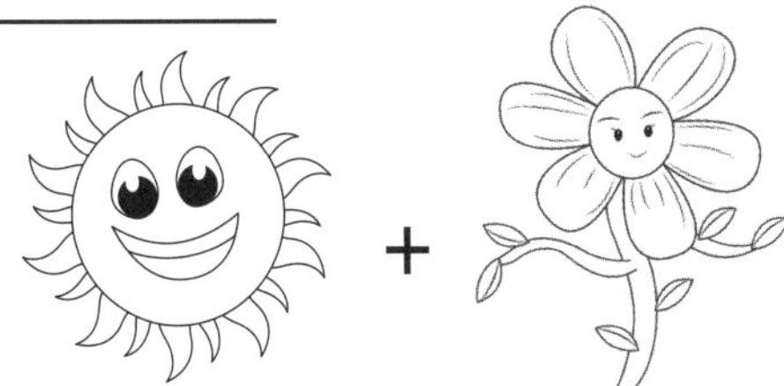

Challenge words

6 Write the word.

everyone

somewhere

newspaper

grasshopper

thunderstorm

skateboard

lifeguard

wheelbarrow

supermarket

honeycomb

7 Word clues. Which challenge word matches?

a small cart

person watching over you while you swim

something made by bees

an insect with wings

a large store

a publication filled with articles and advertisements

all of us

8 Hidden words. Find the the challenge word hidden in these letters.

olehthunderstormhsauo

yeuskateboardouash

sduhysomewhereoihs

asugeveryoneouiha

asidhhoneycombkjgho

kjsghgrasshopperoihad

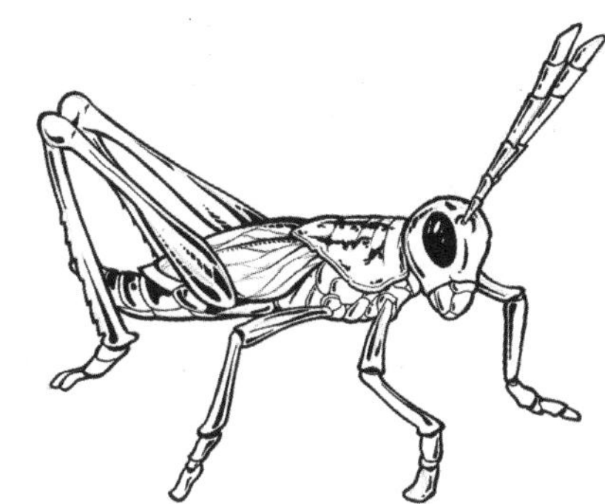

squ, sch and sph words

List

1 Write the word.

squad ____
squat ____
squid ____
squint ____
school ____
sphere ____
square ____
squish ____
squeal ____
squash ____
squirt ____
squiggle ____
sphinx ____
scheme ____
squirrel ____
squeeze ____
squelch ____
squeaky ____
squirm ____
squall ____

2 Sort the words.

Words with *squ*

____ ____
____ ____
____ ____
____ ____
____ ____
____ ____
____ ____
____ ____

Words with *sch*

____ ____

Words with *sph*

____ ____

3 Unscramble these words.

eeezqus ____
rrelqusi ____
oolchs ____
unitsq ____
qusad ____
suatq ____
qusare ____
queaksy ____
elchqus ____
gugliqse ____

4 Name.

____

____

____

____

5 Underline the spelling mistake. Write the word correctly.

Please squert plenty of detergent into the sink. ______

When I blew the whistle, it made a skweaky sound. ______

I had to sqweeze the tomato sauce out of the bottle. ______

I tried to sqwish the annoying mosquito. ______

The girl's piercing sqweal hurt everyone's ears. ______

I tried to sqwash as many clothes as possible into my suitcase. ______

A sqwad of police officers arrived quickly at the scene. ______

The sun's light was so bright it made me sqwint. ______

Our skewl is getting a new library and a new hall. ______

My favourite 3D object is a sfhere. ______

Challenge words

6 Write the word.

squawk ______

scholar ______

squabble ______

squadron ______

squeamish ______

squatter ______

squelchy ______

spherical ______

atmosphere ______

hemisphere ______

7 Hidden words. Find the challenge word.

ncassquabbleioyd ______

msloatmospherejshu ______

sdfgsquawkcasoh ______

aloesquadronobsaj ______

asdhusphericaldfgua ______

uianlsquatteroiadh ______

8 Complete the sentence.

Australia is in the southern ______.

The ball was ______ in shape.

The ______ of fighter jets took off.

9 Word clues. Which challenge word matches?

made sick by unpleasant sights ______

a half of a sphere ______

the gases surrounding a planet ______

describes a squishing or sucking sound ______

a person who studies ______

to quarrel over unimportant matters ______

Suffixes – y

List

1 Write the word.

windy ______
sleepy ______
cloudy ______
rainy ______
tricky ______
dusty ______
creamy ______
fatty ______
muddy ______
easy ______
funny ______
watery ______
stormy ______
thirsty ______
floppy ______
shiny ______
smoky ______
greasy ______
snappy ______
scary ______

2 Unravel these list words.

oludcy ______
nynuf ______
lpopyf ______
tomrsy ______
lsypee ______
krtyic ______

3 Missing letters. Write the missing letters.

cr_____m____ gr_____s____
wa_____y d_____ty
f_____py th_____t____

4 Meaning. Which list word means?

causing laughter or amusement ______
hanging or flapping in a loose way ______
feeling a need to drink ______
quick, rapid or sudden ______

5 Word clue. Which list word matches?

like or looking like smoke ______
covered in dust or powder ______
frightening ______
a great amount of wind ______
covered in mud ______
rain, wind, thunder and lightning ______
difficult ______
polished ______

6 Underline the spelling mistake. Write the word correctly.

On windie days we like to fly our kites. ______

On dark and stormi nights I like to cuddle up in bed. ______

After the rain, our backyard was all mudie. ______

My sister likes to watch scari movies. ______

The kitchen was smokey when Dad burnt the toast. ______

Our homemade yoghurt is soft and creemy. ______

It was a cold and clowdy day. ______

I stayed up late, so I felt quite slepi in the morning. ______

Eating too much fati food will make you sick. ______

Mum's new car was very clean and shiney. ______

Our maths homework was quite trickey. ______

Challenge words

7 Write the word.

healthy ______

sparkly ______

breezy ______

noisy ______

squeaky ______

drowsy ______

woolly ______

spongy ______

spicy ______

prickly ______

8 Complete the sentence.

The ______ meal made her mouth burn.

The sea looked ______ in the sunshine.

The sheep was white and ______.

The door made a ______ sound when it opened.

Salad is a ______ meal.

The cactus had ______ spikes.

The ground was ______ close to the lake.

9 Another way to say it. Which challenge word could replace the underlined word?

The weather was <u>windy</u> and cool. ______

The mattress was <u>springy</u> and comfortable. ______

The dog's bark was <u>loud</u>. ______

He felt <u>sleepy</u> after eating the large meal. ______

The carpet was <u>furry</u> and soft. ______

Contractions

List 1 Write the word.

I'm	______
I'll	______
I've	______
she's	______
they'll	______
what's	______
it's	______
we'll	______
we've	______
that's	______
isn't	______
can't	______
hasn't	______
won't	______
didn't	______
don't	______
who's	______
we're	______
they're	______
o'clock	______

2 Write the matching contraction.

cannot	______
will not	______
they will	______
what is	______
they are	______
we have	______
I will	______
do not	______
I have	______
it is	______

DO NOT DISTURB

3 Rewrite the word with the apostrophe.

Im	______	theyll	______
dont	______	Ill	______
oclock	______	whos	______
hasnt	______	theyre	______
weve	______	didnt	______
thats	______	wont	______
shes	______	were	______

4 Correct contraction. Circle the correct contraction.

what is	what's wha'ts	I have	Iv'e I've	that is	tha'ts that's
we are	w'ere we're	we will	we'll w'ell	will not	won't wo'nt
it is	it's i'ts	cannot	ca'nt can't	has not	hasn't ha'snt
is not	isn't isnt'	she is	she's sh'es	they are	the'yre they're

Contractions

5 Underline the spelling mistake. Write the word correctly.

Im' going to my room. ______

Is'nt it hot today! ______

I was so tired I did'nt want to get out of bed. ______

You should'nt say nasty things about your friends. ______

Wev'e decided to go swimming tomorrow. ______

We will meet at 1 oclo'ck at Avery's place. ______

Do'nt tell me what to do! ______

W'ere going to have a great time! ______

Wha'ts that awful smell coming from your bag? ______

I cant' believe that school is almost over. ______

Challenge words

6 Write the word.

aren't ______

must've ______

doesn't ______

couldn't ______

wouldn't ______

shouldn't ______

would've ______

could've ______

should've ______

might've ______

7 Complete the contraction.

are______

does______

might______

must______

should______

should______

8 Another way to say it. Which challenge word could replace the underlined words?

We <u>must have</u> missed each other by a few minutes. ______

They <u>could have</u> eaten all the pizza, but they saved me a piece. ______

You <u>should not</u> run around the swimming pool. ______

She <u>should have</u> come to the party with you. ______

I <u>could not</u> eat another bite of food. ______

They <u>might have</u> won if they had tried a little harder. ______

Irregular Plurals

List **1 Write the word.**

leaves ____________
roofs ____________
men ____________
mice ____________
sheep ____________
lives ____________
cliffs ____________
wolves ____________
children ____________
music ____________
loaves ____________
chiefs ____________
geese ____________
people ____________
bread ____________
calves ____________
chefs ____________
women ____________
trousers ____________
scarves ____________

2 Make the words plural.

woman ____________
scarf ____________
mouse ____________
calf ____________
man ____________
loaf ____________
life ____________
leaf ____________
chief ____________
person ____________

3 Complete these words with *ves* or *fs.*

loa________
roo________
che________
clif________
cal________
wol________
lea________

4 Name.

____

____

____

____

Irregular Plurals

5 Underline the spelling mistake. Write the word correctly.

I have two pet mouses. ______

The sheeps are in the paddock. ______

The gooses hissed at us. ______

The mans are over there. ______

There were lots of peoples waiting. ______

We bought two loaves of breads. ______

The womans are deciding which tools to bring. ______

The childs are playing outside. ______

He is wearing a new pair of trouser. ______

I listen to different types of musics. ______

Challenge words

6 Write the word.

knives ______

shelves ______

beliefs ______

oases ______

cacti ______

thieves ______

ellipses ______

equipment ______

furniture ______

spectacles ______

7 Complete the sentence.

The ______ stole the expensive jewel.

My grandmother can't see as she has lost her ______ .

The ______ were all different colours, but they were all prickly.

They bought new ______ to go in the family room.

Her ______ were filled with books.

He had strong ______ about animal rights.

8 Word clues. Which list word matches?

areas in a desert where plants grow ______

punctuation marks of three fullstops each ______

tools with sharp, thin blades ______

things needed for a particular task ______

Suffixes – ly

List **1 Write the word.**

sadly ____________
slowly ____________
quickly ____________
suddenly ____________
closely ____________
strongly ____________
surely ____________
happily ____________
hopefully ____________
exactly ____________
carefully ____________
extremely ____________
easily ____________
luckily ____________
heavily ____________
angrily ____________
busily ____________
properly ____________
perfectly ____________
nervously ____________

2 Fill in the missing letters.

s___r___ng ___ ___
___ur___l___
ca___ef ___ ___ ___ ___
e___s___l___
___uck___ ___ ___
an___ ___i___ ___
___a___e___ ___ll___
b___ ___ ___ly
ne___ ___ ___ ___sly
q___i___k___y
su___ ___ ___n___y

3 In a group. Write the list word that belongs in each group.

angry, angrier, ____________
easy, easier, ____________
close, closer, ____________
quick, quicker, ____________
happy, happier, ____________
hope, hopeful, ____________

4 Meaning. Which list word means?

fortunately ____________
unhappily ____________
without fault or mistake ____________
with great movement, force or energy ____________
in a cautious manner ____________
staying nearby ____________
in a cross way ____________
without any speed ____________

Suffixes – ly

5 Write the word in brackets correctly.

(Hopeful) ________________ I'll be able to play next week.

(Sad) ________________ my oldest friend is moving away tomorrow.

We used a magnifying glass to look (close) ________________ at the insect.

(Lucky) ________________ I brought my umbrella with me as it's started raining.

The doctor (careful) ________________ removed the patient's bandages.

He sat down (heavy) ________________ and broke the chair.

I left my brother and sister playing (happy) ________________ in the corner.

I practised until I could play the song (perfect) ________________.

I can (easy) ________________ jump over that fence.

Challenge words

6 Write the word.

noisily ________________

steadily ________________

certainly ________________

wearily ________________

regularly ________________

fortunately ________________

anxiously ________________

definitely ________________

immediately ________________

successfully ________________

7 Hidden words. Find the challenge word.

seffortunatelyasih ________________

asumimmediatelyiywea ________________

ysbjanoisilysado ________________

mpqzlcertainlynsof ________________

lawivregularlyoinsc ________________

crsuccessfullyhgap ________________

8 Word clues. Which challenge word matches?

without any doubt ________________

routinely ________________

right away ________________

loudly ________________

9 Complete with a challenge word.

A word that means the same as now is ________________.

A word that means the opposite of unlucky is ________________.

A word that shows you do something often is ________________.

A word that shows you're worried about something is ________________.

A word that means you've done something well is ________________.

Trigraph – ear

List **1 Write the word.**

ear ____
near ____
bear ____
fear ____
wear ____
hear ____
pear ____
year ____
dear ____
gear ____
shear ____
earn ____
clear ____
earth ____
learn ____
swear ____
smear ____
spear ____
yearly ____
heart ____

2 Word clues. Which list word matches?

a body part you hear with ____
a fruit ____
365 days ____
our planet ____
a long stick with a sharp point ____
the part of your body that pumps blood ____

3 Unscramble these words.

frae	____	yrae	____
aerw	____	rean	____
aher	____	rae	____
raed	____	yyealr	____
rgea	____	earnl	____
heasr	____	arews	____
caerl	____	aerms	____
raep	____	thaer	____
raeps	____	raeb	____
rane	____	htrae	____

4 Meaning. Which list word means?

12 months ____
to remove wool from an animal ____
not blocked, open ____
cogs on a bicycle ____
to spread on or over a surface ____
to get money ____
a sweet, bell-shaped fruit ____
fright or worry ____
close by ____

Trigraph – ear

5 Fill in the missing word.

The hunter threw his s______________ but it missed its target.

I like to sit n______________ the window to get some fresh air.

The hikers stood still as a huge grizzly b______________ walked past them.

She whispered her secret in my e______________.

Venus is the closest planet to e______________.

This summer I am going to l______________ how to juggle.

I grabbed an apple and a p______________ from the fruit bowl.

He has a f______________ of heights.

Please speak up as I can't h______________ what you're saying.

Challenge words

6 Write the word.

beard ______________

earring ______________

pearl ______________

dreary ______________

heard ______________

weary ______________

nearby ______________

appear ______________

hearth ______________

search ______________

7 Word clues. Which challenge word matches?

tired ______________

round object from an oyster ______________

listened ______________

jewellery worn in the earlobe ______________

the floor of a fireplace ______________

not far away ______________

facial hair ______________

to become visible ______________

to look for something ______________

gloomy or dull ______________

8 Another way to say it. Which challenge word could replace the underlined word?

The man shaved his <u>stubble</u> off as it was itchy. ______________

The pirates went on a <u>hunt</u> for the buried treasure. ______________

The owners of the <u>neighbouring</u> house were very friendly. ______________

We stayed indoors on the grey, <u>bleak</u> day. ______________

The magician made a rabbit <u>materialize</u> in his hat. ______________

We were <u>exhausted</u> after our long hike. ______________

Prefixes – un, dis, mis

List

unable
disagree
mislead
unfair
dislike
unload
unlock
uncover
uneven
unhappy
unpleasant
disappear
misbehave
unknown
mistreat
unhealthy
mismatch
unusual
unwrap
unlucky

1 Write the word.

2 Sort the words.

un	*dis*	*mis*

3 Chunks. Rearrange the syllables to make a list word.

be-mis-have
pleas-ant-un
u-un-al-us
gree-dis-a
ch-mat-mis
ap-dis-pear

4 Meaning. Which list word means?

not normal
to vanish
to treat badly
to have a different opinion
reveal
to cause someone to believe something that is not true

5 Complete the missing word.

She was un________________ to visit her friend because she had a cold.

You could mis________________ people if you don't be honest and open.

The secret agent was trying to un________________ the enemy's master plan.

We got excited when the rain clouds began to dis________________.

I like to mis________________ my socks and wear one blue and one green one.

We held our noses because of the un________________ smell.

I usually dis________________ with my brother, but this time he was absolutely right.

We can't know everything; some things remain un________________ .

Challenge words

6 Write the word.

disbelief ________________

dishonest ________________

disapprove ________________

unnecessary ________________

unfamiliar ________________

misunderstanding ________________

unexpected ________________

misplace ________________

disconnect ________________

uncertain ________________

7 Hidden words. Find the challenge word.

uydnunfamiliarueyn ________________

auendishonestaiyn ________________

asyguncertaineuabj ________________

asdsdisapprovejsaih ________________

asermisplaceihyke ________________

asduncertainseioy ________________

rtrodisconnectklps ________________

rmisunderstandingx ________________

mnounnecessarylsto ________________

opdisbelieffste ________________

8 Complete the sentence.

She shook her head in ________________.

Their argument started with a simple ________________.

When there is a storm, we always ________________ the computer.

His visit was an ________________ event.

He is a ________________ boy who always tells lies.

Tricky words

List **1 Write the word.**

before ____
where ____
every ____
once ____
does ____
didn't ____
friends ____
let's ____
its ____
it's ____
quiet ____
clothes ____
minute ____
forward ____
group ____
difficult ____
people ____
often ____
another ____
together ____

2 Write the list words in alphabetical order.

____ ____
____ ____
____ ____
____ ____
____ ____
____ ____
____ ____
____ ____
____ ____
____ ____

3 Fill in the missing letters.

____h____r____
d____f____ic____lt
e____e____y
____e____ore
____og____t____er
o____c____
d____dn'____
____ri____nd____
o____t____n
____oe____
____e____'s
i____s
it'____
c____ot____e____
f____ ____w____rd
____n____th____r

4 Meaning. Which list word means?

towards the direction that is in front of you ____
at an earlier time ____
hard to do or understand ____
a number of people or things ____
making no sound or noise ____
only one time ____
sixty seconds ____
companions ____

Tricky words

5 Underline the spelling mistake. Write the word correctly.

I find it dificult to make hard decisions. ____________

Our dog is not very friendly towards other poeple. ____________

We offten go to the park to kick a football. ____________

I was so full I couldn't eat anuther bite. ____________

Hailey and Jimmy work really well togetha. ____________

I packed my clouths into a suitcase. ____________

Challenge words

6 Write the word.

because ____________

really ____________

poetry ____________

beautiful ____________

different ____________

interesting ____________

February ____________

island ____________

opposite ____________

surprise ____________

7 Word clues. Which challenge word matches?

pretty ____________

second month ____________

surrounded by water ____________

to catch off guard ____________

for that reason ____________

as different as possible ____________

something you read or recite ____________

not the same ____________

8 Another way to say it. Which challenge word could replace the underlined words?

They were running late <u>as</u> traffic was bad. ____________

My birthday is in <u>the second month of the year</u>. ____________

I found the colours of the sky <u>intriguing</u>. ____________

It was a <u>shock</u> to see my grandparents at my house. ____________

The boys have <u>contrasting</u> opinions about the book. ____________

The <u>piece of land</u> was covered in sand and palm trees. ____________

Her new dress was very <u>pretty</u>. ____________

The stories are <u>not the same</u>. ____________

Suffixes – ness

List **1 Write the word.**

darkness ______
goodness ______
kindness ______
stillness ______
sickness ______
brightness ______
sweetness ______
softness ______
slowness ______
greatness ______
happiness ______
emptiness ______
forgiveness ______
readiness ______
wickedness ______
foolishness ______
carelessness ______
eagerness ______
nastiness ______
sharpness ______

2 Word building. Add the suffix to the base words.

foolish ______
careless ______
eager ______
bright ______
sharp ______
slow ______
good ______
dark ______

3 Chunks. Rearrange the letters to make a list word.

ft ne ss so ______
ti ne ss nas ______
nd ne ss ki ______
ill ss ne st ______
ss ee sw t ne ______
eat ss ne gr ______
pi hap ss ne ______
ss ne giv for e ______
ss di rea ne ______
ck ed ne ss wi ______

4 Name.

e______

s______

s______

s______

5 Underline the spelling mistake. Write the word correctly.

I like the sweteness of honey. ____________

He is filled with wikednes. ____________

I blinked because of the briteness of the light. ____________

She is laughing with happynes. ____________

The opposite of fullness is emptynes. ____________

Her egernes is a pleasure to watch. ____________

His knives are known for their sharpniss. ____________

The sloeness of a sloth is amazing. ____________

Kinedniss is a wonderful quality to have. ____________

His cairlisness will get him into trouble. ____________

Challenge words

6 Write the word.

seriousness ____________

usefulness ____________

selfishness ____________

awkwardness ____________

loneliness ____________

cleanliness ____________

friendliness ____________

restlessness ____________

forgetfulness ____________

consciousness ____________

7 Word clues. Which challenge word matches?

welcoming to others ____________

likely to forget ____________

clumsiness ____________

awake and aware ____________

worried only about yourself ____________

feeling alone ____________

not dirty ____________

importance ____________

handy ____________

8 Hidden words. Find the challenge word.

asucleanlinessyand ____________

sihfforgetfulnessaosiy ____________

vnjdusefulnessirute ____________

rongrestlessnessobep ____________

aqpbefriendlinessihikk ____________

fydndseriousnessuysho ____________

RULES AND GENERALISATIONS

Plurals

s, es
Add *s* to many nouns to make a plural, cat → cats.
Nouns that end in *s, sh, ch, x* and *z*, add *es*, fox → *foxes*.
Some nouns that end in *o* use *es*, tomato → *tomatoes*.

es
Words end in *consonant* + *y*, change the *y* to *i* and add es, copy → *copies*.
Words end in *vowel* + *y*, just add *s*, donkey → *donkeys*.

Irregular plurals
Some nouns that end in *f* or *fe*, change *f* or *fe* to *v* before adding *es*, thief → *thieves*.
Some nouns change in other ways, tooth → *teeth*.
Some nouns don't change at all, one fish → *five fish*.

Suffixes

ed, d
For past tense verbs add *ed*, walk → *walked*.
When a verb ends in *e*, just add *d*, bake → *baked*.
If the verb ends with a *short vowel* + *consonant*, double the consonant then add *ed*, sip → *sipped*.
If the verb ends in *y*, change the *y* to *i* and add *ed*, worry → *worried*.
Irregular verbs do not use *ed* in the past tense, grow → *grew*, bite → *bit*, see → *saw*.

ing
For many verbs just add *ing*, cook → *cooking*.
When a verb ends in *e*, drop the e before adding *ing*, write → *writing*.
If the verb ends with a *short vowel* + *consonant*, double the consonant then add *ing*, shop → *shopping*.

Prefixes

un, dis, mis
The prefix *un*, *dis* or *mis* turns a word into its opposite.
true → *untrue*   approve → *disapprove*   print → *misprint*

Contractions

Contractions use an apostrophe (’) to replace some letters.
you are → you’re   that will → that’ll   are not → aren’t

Homophones

Homophones are words that sound the same but are spelled differently and have different meanings.
wood → would   piece → peace   stair → stare